D0119147

DISCARD

The Boston Tea Party

by Ann Malaspina

Content Consultant
Robert J. Allison, Professor of History
Suffolk University

CARLSBAD
CITY LIBRARY
Carlsbad, CA
92011

CORE
LIBRARY

J973.3115
MAL

Published by ABDO Publishing Company, PO Box 398166, Minneapolis, MN 55439. Copyright © 2013 by Abdo Consulting Group, Inc. International copyrights reserved in all countries. No part of this book may be reproduced in any form without written permission from the publisher. The Core Library™ is a trademark and logo of ABDO Publishing Company.

Printed in the United States of America,
North Mankato, Minnesota
112012
012013

♻ THIS BOOK CONTAINS AT LEAST 10% RECYCLED MATERIALS.

Editor: Blythe Hurley
Series Designer: Becky Daum

Cataloging-in-Publication Data
Malaspina, Ann.
 The Boston Tea Party / Ann Malaspina.
   p. cm. -- (Foundations of our nation)
Includes bibliographical references and index.
ISBN 978-1-61783-707-4
1. Boston Tea Party, 1773--Juvenile literature.   I. Title.
973.3/115--dc22

                                        2012914475

Photo Credits: North Wind/North Wind Picture Archives, cover, 1, 9, 12, 17, 22, 28, 31, 33, 36, 40, 45; iStockphoto/Thinkstock, 4; Public Domain, 6; Interim Archives/Getty Images, 11; Time Life Pictures/Mansell/Time Life Pictures/Getty Images, 15; Hulton Archive/Getty Images, 19, 26

Cover: Colonists threw British tea into Boston Harbor. This event became know as the Boston Tea Party.

JUNE 2013

CONTENTS

CHAPTER ONE
Ship in the Harbor **4**

CHAPTER TWO
The Dreaded Tea Tax **12**

CHAPTER THREE
Resistance on Both Sides **22**

CHAPTER FOUR
"A Little Saltwater Tea" **28**

CHAPTER FIVE
Turning Point **36**

Important Dates 42

Stop and Think 44

Glossary 46

Learn More 47

Index 48

About the Author 48

Ship in the Harbor

On November 28, 1773, a ship called the *Dartmouth* sailed into Boston Harbor. Captain James Hall and his crew had crossed the Atlantic Ocean from England. One hundred and fourteen chests of tea sat in the ship's hold. The captain had 20 days to unload the tea and pay the duty, or tax, owed on it.

Boston Harbor today. This peaceful scene was once the setting for the Boston Tea Party.

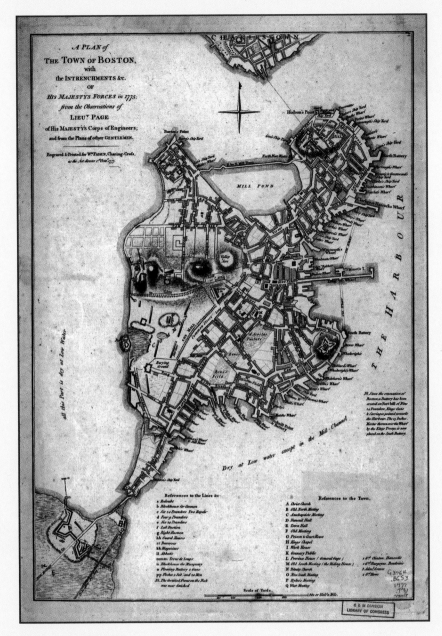

Boston in 1775

This map of Boston was made by a British army officer in 1775. Why would the British need a detailed map of Boston at that time? Colonists also made maps of Boston. Why would the British want one created by their own mapmaker?

Word of the ship's arrival raced through the streets of Boston. The *Dartmouth* was an American ship. But the British East India Company owned the tea. This company was important to Great Britain.

Colonists had to pay a tax on East India Company tea. The extra money went to the British government. The colonists felt this was unfair. Colonial merchants were only allowed to sell this tea. If they sold tea from other sources they would be forced out of business. Angry colonists wanted the ship to go back to Great Britain.

The town board met to decide what to do. The board's elected officials hoped to talk the ship's owner into turning the *Dartmouth* around.

Trouble Brewing

Boston's Sons of Liberty was a group formed by colonists to protest what they saw as the abuse of their rights by Great Britain. The Sons of Liberty thought of themselves as patriots. They had tried to stop the tea from coming to Boston for weeks.

Sons of Liberty

Were the Sons of Liberty criminals or heroes? Or were they ordinary colonists who wanted fair treatment from the British? This secret political group led many protests against the British government's laws and taxes in the years leading up to the American Revolution. By the end of 1765, Sons of Liberty chapters had spread throughout the colonies. Their protests often turned violent. They frequently destroyed property.

Samuel Adams was a leader of many anti-British protests. He was determined to keep British tea out of Boston. Adams had fought against British taxes and tyranny for years. Now that the tea had arrived, Adams and other angry colonists had to decide what to do. Patriots put up signs all over Boston inviting colonists to a meeting to discuss the problem.

Loyalists Wait for the Tea

A handful of colonial merchants in Boston waited for the tea. They had the support of the Massachusetts colony governor, Thomas Hutchinson. He was a firm

Samuel Adams was a leading Boston patriot.

Loyalist. Three members of his family were among the men chosen to sell the tea shipment.

Other merchants felt differently. John Hancock was a merchant and a respected leader in the colonial government. He was also very rich. People thought some of his fortune had come from smuggling goods into the colonies on his ships. Smuggling was common at that time because it allowed colonists to avoid paying taxes. One of the items often smuggled

The Liberty Tree

Colonists planted elm trees to provide shade in Boston in 1646. One tree near Boston Common grew particularly tall and strong. The Sons of Liberty gathered at the tree to protest the Stamp Act in 1765. People began calling it the Liberty Tree. Other towns in the colonies soon had their own. Patriots gathered under their spreading branches to discuss issues and protest British taxes and policies. British soldiers cut down Boston's Liberty Tree in 1775. But they couldn't stop the fight for independence. Today, a marker shows where the Liberty Tree once stood.

into the colonies was Dutch tea. The cheaper East India Company tea would hurt Hancock's business.

The *Dartmouth* sat in Boston Harbor for almost three weeks. It was guarded by men from the Sons of Liberty group, who did not want the tea to be unloaded. Soon, two more East India Company tea ships would also arrive.

A colonial figure standing under the Liberty Tree, a
rallying place for American patriots.

CHAPTER TWO

The Dreaded Tea Tax

Tea was not just a hot drink to colonists. It also became a symbol of Great Britain's unfair treatment of the American colonies. How did a popular drink become a symbol of British injustice? It began after the British won the French and Indian War.

Great Britain won this war, which began in 1754 and ended in 1763. But nine years of fighting had

Colonists in Boston rioted to protest the Stamp Act.

Smuggling

Some colonial merchants grew rich by smuggling goods into the colonies. They were able to sell products at lower prices. This was because they did not pay taxes on them. Products from molasses to tea were hidden in ship holds. Ships landed in smaller harbors or in the dead of night to avoid customs officers. After colonists boycotted, or refused to buy, British tea, smugglers provided Dutch tea. Smuggling brought wealth to the American colonies. One of John Hancock's ships, the *Liberty*, was seized in June 1768. British officials suspected cases of wine were hidden on board. This caused a riot at the harbor.

drained their treasury. Great Britain still needed to keep an army in the colonies. Paying for the soldiers was expensive. It cost money to govern the colonies. Great Britain wanted the colonies to help pay the bills.

The Stamp Act

Parliament decided to make the American colonists pay their share of these costs through taxes. The Sugar Act in 1764 created taxes on molasses, coffee, fabric, and other goods. The new law hurt traders and merchants.

Benjamin Franklin possibly drew this 1767 political cartoon. It warns how the Stamp Act could affect the colonies.

In 1765 the British government passed the Stamp Act. Every printed paper had to have an official stamp, which cost extra money. Colonists had to pay more for newspapers, marriage licenses, and other important documents. Only a few people had been affected by taxes in the past. But the Stamp Act affected all colonists.

The colonists were outraged. They did not have a representative in Parliament, which made

Great Britain's laws. They felt that taxation without representation was unfair. The British government did not think the colonists needed a representative in Parliament. They believed that Parliament could make decisions for them. The colonists were British citizens. They should obey British laws and pay taxes.

Anger at the Stamp Act grew in Boston. The Sons of Liberty hung an effigy, or dummy, of British stamp official Andrew Oliver on a branch on August 14, 1765. The crowd later tore apart Oliver's warehouse and home.

Colonists hung more dummies from trees. Protests spread. Mobs attacked tax collectors in other colonies. Colonists refused to buy British goods. They even organized a Stamp Act Congress to protest the hated tax.

The British government began to see it would cost more to enforce the Stamp Act than it would earn in taxes. Parliament repealed the act on March 18, 1766. But at the same time, Parliament passed a

An effigy of Andrew Oliver was hung by protesting colonists in 1765.

law called the Declaratory Act. This law stated that Parliament had the power to govern and tax the colonies however it chose. Great Britain had not given up on taxing the colonists.

Parliament passed new laws called the Townshend Acts in June 1767. New taxes were put in place on everyday items such as lead, glass, paint, paper, and tea. Soldiers were sent to Boston to enforce these new taxes. Again, colonists protested and agreed not to buy British goods.

Relations between the colonists and Great Britain grew worse. Fights often broke out between soldiers and colonists in Boston. In 1770 British soldiers fired on a crowd of colonists who had been harassing them on a Boston street. The soldiers killed five and injured six. This event was called the Boston Massacre.

Great Britain repealed the Townshend Acts in April 1770, except for the tax on tea. People called this tax "the dreaded tea tax." Many colonists refused to drink British tea in protest.

The Tea Act

Three years later a new British law, the Tea Act of 1773, added fuel to the colonists' anger. This act was created to save the British East India Company. It was one of the largest corporations in the world at the time. The Tea Act included a new rule that said the company did not have to pay taxes to import tea from

A Boston colonist reads a royal proclamation about the Tea Act.

China. In the colonies, only Loyalist merchants could sell this tea.

The Tea Act brought the price of tea down. But it also allowed Great Britain to control trade in the colonies. With this new law, Great Britain proved it could still tax the colonies. The colonists were furious.

Seven Ships Fuel the Fire

The East India Company's warehouses were overflowing with unsold tea. In October 1773, seven ships left London with hundreds of chests of this tea on board. Four were bound for Boston. The others headed to Charleston, Philadelphia, and New York. News of the ships traveled quickly. On October 18, the *Boston Gazette* announced the tea was on its way. The newspaper urged colonists "to destroy it."

FURTHER EVIDENCE

New taxes and laws created by the British government angered the American colonists. Review Chapter Two. What was its main point? What evidence was given to support that point? Visit the Web site below to learn more about how one patriot, Samuel Adams, spoke out against the Tea Act. Find a quote that supports this chapter's main point.

Samuel Adams
www.masshist.org/education/resources/blackington/samuel_adams.pdf

British Acts Leading Up to the Boston Tea Party, 1764–1773

The British government hoped to both raise money and control the colonies with the Stamp Act and other new laws. Instead, these acts inspired protests and rebellion among colonists. Would you have voted for the Stamp Act if you were a member of the British Parliament? Why or why not? What else could the British government have done to achieve its goals?

Year	Act	What Did It Do?	What Was the Result?
1764	The Sugar Act	Lowered taxes on sugar, coffee, and other non-British goods exported to the American colonies but required enforcement.	Colonial merchants lost business and trading opportunities.
1764	The Currency Act	Banned colonists from printing paper money.	Colonists lost the right to control their own currency.
1765	The Quartering Act	Forced colonists to provide British troops with housing and supplies.	Colonists were angered by this burden.
1765	The Stamp Act	Required an official stamp on newspapers, diplomas, broadsides, legal documents, and many other printed papers.	Violent protests erupted over this taxation without representation by Parliament. The Stamp Act was canceled.
1767	The Townshend Acts	Added taxes on glass, lead, paint, paper, tea, and other everyday items imported from Great Britain.	Colonists boycotted British goods. British troops were sent in an attempt to control rebellious colonists. The taxes were repealed (except for the tea tax).
1773	The Tea Act	Gave the British East India Company and its merchants a monopoly over other colonial tea merchants.	Outrage over the British monopoly on tea helped to spark the Boston Tea Party on December 16, 1773.

CHAPTER THREE

Resistance on Both Sides

The Green Dragon Tavern was a popular meeting place for the Sons of Liberty and other patriots. They could talk freely without fear of Loyalists overhearing them. One night in early November 1773, a group of patriots sat at a table. They knew that the ships bringing British tea were only weeks away from American shores. How would they stop the tea from being sold in the colonies?

This Boston site, shown in the 1800s, is close to where the Boston Tea Party was planned.

Women and Resistance

Women played a key role in resisting British taxes. They refused to buy British tea for their families. Instead, they made tea from raspberry bush leaves or served coffee and hot chocolate. Abigail Adams, wife of lawyer John Adams, went to the anti-tea meetings at the Old South Meeting House.

The men voted on a resolution to prevent the tea from coming ashore. They sent letters to the merchants who planned to sell the East India Company tea. These letters asked the merchants to appear at the Liberty Tree. The patriots wanted to convince them to refuse the tea. The merchants were Loyalists, but they were also American colonists. The patriots believed that for the good of the colonies, these merchants must not sell the British company's tea.

Mob Rule

On November 3, 500 people met at the Liberty Tree. The colonists waited for the tea merchants. Enraged, the crowd moved to the building where the merchants were. The merchants told the people they would not bow to the will of a mob.

The colonists refused to give up. A special town meeting was called at Faneuil Hall. Town hall meetings were the local governing body of Boston. Hancock was the moderator. The colonists voted for a resolution calling for opposition to the sale of the tea. They appointed a committee to demand that the tea merchants resign. This would mean there would be no one to sell the British tea.

The merchants would not agree. In the days that followed, some of the merchants received violent threats. But the merchants still wanted to do business with the British and sell the tea.

Tea Arrives

On November 28, the first tea ship, the *Dartmouth*, arrived in Boston. The next day, about 5,000 people met at the Old South Meeting House. The colonists demanded that the ship go back to London. They

An artist's vision of Loyalist governor Thomas Hutchinson escaping from rioters who attacked his home while they protested the Stamp Act

ordered men to guard the *Dartmouth* to make sure the tea was not unloaded.

Loyalist Governor

The *Dartmouth*'s owner, Francis Rotch, was caught in the middle. The patriots wouldn't let him unload the tea, and customs officials wouldn't let the ship leave without delivering its cargo.

Hutchinson, the Loyalist governor, was the one man who might have been able to end the crisis. Even though he loved the American colonies, Hutchinson was not sympathetic to the patriots. They didn't like him either.

Rebellious colonists had attacked Hutchinson's house after the Stamp Act passed. The Massachusetts Assembly had published his private letters, in which he expressed his Loyalist views. The assembly had even asked Great Britain to remove him as governor. Why should he help the patriots? His job was to follow the wishes of the king. He ordered that no ships were to leave Boston Harbor.

EXPLORE ONLINE

During the events leading to the Boston Tea Party, colonial newspapers kept people informed about the rising tensions between the patriots and the British. Often, these newspaper stories were based on opinions instead of facts. Go to the Web site below, and read some of these stories. Decide for yourself if the writers were reporting facts, opinions, or some of both.

The Boston Tea Party
www.masshist.org/revolution/teaparty.php

CHAPTER FOUR

"A Little Saltwater Tea"

By December 15, 1773, two more ships full of British tea were in Boston Harbor. Members of the Sons of Liberty stood on the wharf watching day and night. Only days remained for the *Dartmouth*'s tea to be unloaded and the duty to be paid.

At ten o'clock in the morning on December 16, a crowd of more than 5,000 people filled the balconies and aisles of the Old South Meeting House. It was the last day for the *Dartmouth*'s owner to either unload the tea or start the *Dartmouth* back to Great Britain. Otherwise, the British government would seize the tea.

In a last effort to end the crisis, the patriots sent Rotch to ask Hutchinson once more to allow the ship to leave Boston. Hutchinson refused. Rotch said that he could do no more.

"A Mob! A Mob!"

The crowd erupted. "Boston Harbor a teapot tonight!" some people yelled. A band of men appeared at the door. They wore ragged clothes and blankets. Dabs of paint, coal dust, and mud hid their faces. They looked like American Indians and shouted war whoops and whistles. "The Mohawks are come!" some people cried. Others called out, "A mob! A mob!"

People poured into the streets and headed to Griffin's Wharf. As night fell, men climbed aboard the

Colonists disguised as American Indians opened tea chests with tomahawks and dumped the tea overboard.

Dartmouth. More men ran to join them from a nearby hill. Still others joined in at the last minute. There may have been 100 to 200 men in all, carrying muskets and bayonets.

Tea Overboard

The men worked silently and quickly. Guards were posted to keep watch for the British. No one knew if or when the British soldiers would try to stop them. Once on board the *Dartmouth*, the men ordered the crew and customs officers to shore. Using ropes and weights, they lifted the wooden tea chests onto the deck. Each weighed 400 pounds. Men swung axes and tomahawks to break them open.

More men climbed onto the two other ships that had brought British tea to Boston. In total, they threw 342 tea chests into the harbor, destroying more than 90,000 pounds (about 41,000 kg) of tea. The East India Company later claimed the tea was worth more than 9,659 British pounds sterling—more than $1 million in today's money.

Three Hours

Townspeople watched in silence from the wharf. Tea leaves piled high in the low tide. One man later told his wife, "We have only been making a little saltwater tea." It took the men about three hours to dump all the tea.

It took the colonists about three hours to dump the tea into Boston Harbor.

The Destruction of the *Peggy Stewart*

Other tea parties sprang up across the colonies in 1773 and 1774. Patriots sunk tea in harbors and burned tea in bonfires. In October 1774, the ship *Peggy Stewart* arrived in Maryland with a cargo of British tea. The ship owner, Anthony Stewart, angered the colonists when he paid duties on the tea. They did not want any British goods to enter the colonies. Within days, a mob gathered and demanded that Stewart destroy the ship and the tea. Fearing for his life, Stewart set his own ship and the tea chests on fire.

What they had done was against the law and a challenge to the king and Parliament.

The patriots did not consider the Tea Party to be vandalism or theft. Rather, they felt that they had sent an important message to the British government. The colonies would not tolerate the British government's unfair taxes and attempts to control their trade.

John Adams's Diary

In Adams's diary entry from December 17, 1773, he describes his feelings the day after the Boston Tea Party.

Last Night 3 Cargoes of Bohea Tea were emptied into the Sea. This Morning a Man of War sails. This is the most magnificent Movement of all. There is a Dignity, a Majesty, a Sublimity, in this last Effort of the Patriots, that I greatly admire. The People should never rise, without doing something to be remembered—something notable And striking. This Destruction of the Tea is so bold, so daring, so firm, intrepid and inflexible, and it must have so important Consequences, and so lasting, that I cant but consider it as an Epocha in History.

Source: John Adams diary 19, 16 December 1772 – 18 December 1773 [electronic edition], Adams Family Papers: An Electronic Archive, Massachusetts Historical Society, http://www.masshist.org/digitaladams/

Consider Your Audience

Review this passage closely. Consider how you would adapt it for a different audience, such as your parents, your principal, or your younger friends. Write a blog post conveying this same information to your audience. Write it so it can be understood by them. What is the most effective way to get your point across? How does your blog post differ from Adams's diary entry, and why?

CHAPTER FIVE

Turning Point

In the months after the Tea Party, rebellion began to spread through the colonies like a wave. After learning what happened in Boston, the governor of New York advised an East India Company tea ship not to land in New York Harbor. In Pennsylvania, 8,000 protestors turned away the tea ship *Polly* on Christmas Day. The ship sailed back to Great Britain with 697 chests of tea.

George III was king of England during the Boston Tea Party and the American Revolution.

In the next months, patriots burned or seized tea in towns from Maine to South Carolina. They attacked officials. Many colonists continued to boycott tea.

A Challenge to the King

News of the Tea Party reached London in January 1774. British leaders were furious. The Tea Party was not just a protest. It was a challenge to the king and Parliament. King George III would not stand for it.

Coercive Acts

Parliament passed harsh new laws in 1774 to punish Boston. These laws were known as the Coercive Acts. The first was the Boston Port Act. This law closed the town's harbor to almost all ship traffic. The port would open again only when Boston paid for the destroyed tea and the taxes owed on it.

Another law called the Massachusetts Government Act gave the Loyalist governor authority over Boston's colonial government. Now only the king could select leaders. Town meetings could not be held without the governor's permission.

Another law allowed British soldiers to live in colonists' homes. To make sure Boston obeyed the new laws, the king sent British soldiers to occupy the town.

The British hoped the Coercive Acts would restore order. But the colonists called them the Intolerable Acts. *Intolerable* means unbearable. Instead of frightening the colonists, these laws fed the spirit of rebellion.

Turning Point

The Boston Tea Party was a turning point in the struggle between

When Was the Tea Party Named the Tea Party?

The phrase "Boston Tea Party" was first used a half century after it happened. Joshua Wyeth, a blacksmith's apprentice in 1773, gave an interview to a reporter during the 1820s. He said he had helped throw the tea overboard that night. The reporter wrote that Wyeth "often boasts of the 'Boston tea party.'" People then began using the phrase to describe the events of that night.

British warships in Boston Harbor in 1774. British soldiers occupied Boston after the Boston Tea Party in an attempt to control the angry colonists.

American colonists and Great Britain. After Parliament's harsh punishment of Boston, many colonists who had been hesitant to break ties with Great Britain changed their minds.

Soon events led to war. On April 18, 1775, Paul Revere warned colonists that 700 British troops were being sent to destroy colonists' weapons stored in nearby Concord. After the sun rose, shots rang out in Lexington and Concord. The American Revolution had begun.

"An Act to Block Up Boston Harbour"

This act was Great Britain's response to the events of the Boston Tea Party. The new law, enacted by Parliament, closed Boston Harbor, harming Boston's economy and citizens.

WHEREAS dangerous commotions and insurrections have been fomented and raised in the town of Boston . . . in which commotions and insurrections certain valuable cargoes of teas . . . were seized and destroyed. . . . And whereas, in the present condition of the said town and harbour, the commerce of his Majesty's subjects cannot be safely carried on there, nor the customs payable to his Majesty duly collected . . . it shall not be lawful for any person or persons whatsoever to lade or put . . . into any ship . . . any goods . . . or to take up . . . any goods . . . upon pain of the forfeiture of the said goods . . . and of the said boat.

Source: Broadside. Sold by Mills and Hicks at printing office in School-Street, Boston, 1774. Massachusetts Historical Society.

Nice View

Compare this section from "An Act to Block Up Boston Harbour" with the quote from John Adams's diary in Chapter Four. Think about both authors' points of view. Write a short essay that explains the point of view of each document. How are they similar and why? How are they different and why?

IMPORTANT DATES

1763

The French and Indian War ends. Great Britain wins the war.

1765

Parliament passes the Stamp Act on March 22. This taxes all printed paper in the American colonies. Protests erupt.

1773

The Tea Act goes into effect in May.

1773

The owner of the *Dartmouth* is denied permission to leave harbor on December 16. Patriots throw the tea overboard.

1774

News of the tea's destruction reaches London in January.

1774

Harsh new laws are passed to punish Boston. Colonists call them the Intolerable Acts.

1773

Boston patriots demand that the tea merchants resign on November 3. The merchants refuse.

1773

The first tea ship, the *Dartmouth*, arrives in Boston Harbor on November 28.

1773

Patriots meet at the Old South Meeting House on November 29 and decide that the tea must go back to England.

1774

Parliament passes the Boston Port Act, closing Boston Harbor until the destroyed tea is paid for.

1774

Parliament places Massachusetts under military rule in June. British troops arrive to restore order.

1775

Paul Revere takes his famous ride on April 18 to warn of the British arrival.

Take a Stand

This book discusses the Boston merchants who sold the British East India Company tea. Take a position on whether they should have agreed to sell the tea or refused to do so. Write a short essay detailing your opinion, reasons for your opinion, and facts and details that support those reasons.

You Are There

Imagine you were in the crowd at Griffin's Wharf on the night of December 16, 1773. Write 300 words describing what you saw and heard. What did the men disguised as American Indians look like? What sounds did their axes and tomahawks make as the tea chests were broken? Was it dark or did the new moon and lanterns help light the night?

Tell the Tale

This book discusses the story of the Boston Tea Party. Write 200 words from the point of view of one of the men who participated in the Boston Tea Party. Why did he decide to risk everything to go to Griffin's Wharf? What did he think and feel as the tea fell into the harbor? Be sure to set the scene, develop a sequence of events, and write a conclusion.

Say What?

Find five words in this book you've never seen or heard before. Find out what they mean. Write the meanings in your own words. Use the words in a sentence about your own life.

GLOSSARY

boycott
to refuse to do something in order to show disapproval

duty
a tax on goods brought into a country or territory

effigy
an image or dummy of something, especially a person

Loyalist
a person who was loyal to Great Britain

Parliament
the government body that makes laws in Great Britain before or during the American Revolution

patriot
a person who loves his or her country and acts for its interests

rebel
someone who is against or fights authority, especially his or her government

smuggle
to move goods secretly, often to avoid paying taxes

tax
money paid to the government for goods or services

tyranny
abuse or cruelty by a government power

LEARN MORE

Books

Cook, Peter. *You Wouldn't Want to Be at the Boston Tea Party! Wharf Water Tea You'd Rather Not Drink*. Danbury, CT: Franklin Watts, 2006. Print.

Freedman, Russell. *The Boston Tea Party*. New York: Holiday House, 2012. Print.

Walker, Ida. *The Boston Tea Party*. Edina, MN: ABDO Publishing, 2008. Print.

Web Links

To learn more about the Boston Tea Party, visit ABDO Publishing Company online at **www.abdopublishing.com**. Web sites about the Boston Tea Party are featured on our Book Links page. These links are routinely monitored and updated to provide the most current information available. Visit **www.mycorelibrary.com** for free additional tools for teachers and students.

INDEX

Adams, Abigail, 24
Adams, John, 24, 35, 41
Adams, Samuel, 8, 20
American Revolution,
  8, 40

Boston Harbor, 5, 10,
  27, 29–30, 38, 41
Boston Massacre, 18
Boston Port Act, 38

Coercive Acts, 38–39

Dartmouth, 5, 7, 10,
  25–26, 29–32
Declaratory Act, 17

East India Company,
  7, 10, 18, 20–21, 24,
  32, 37

Faneuil Hall, 25

French and Indian War,
  13

Green Dragon Tavern,
  23
Griffin's Wharf, 30

Hancock, John, 9–10,
  14, 25
Hutchinson, Thomas, 8,
  26–27, 30

King George III, 38

Liberty, 14
Liberty Tree, 10, 24
Loyalists, 8–9, 19,
  23–24, 26–27, 38

Massachusetts
  Government Act, 38

Old South Meeting
  House, 24–25, 30
Oliver, Andrew, 16

Parliament, 14–17, 21,
  34, 38, 40, 41

Revere, Paul, 40
Rotch, Francis, 26, 30

smuggling, 9, 14
Sons of Liberty, 7–8, 10,
  16, 23, 29
Stamp Act, 10, 14–16,
  21, 27
Sugar Act, 14, 21

taxes, 5, 7–9, 10, 14–21,
  24, 34, 38
Tea Act, 18–21
Townshend Acts, 17–18,
  21

ABOUT THE AUTHOR

Ann Malaspina has written many books about history for young people. She loves to write about Boston, where she had her first job as a reporter for a weekly newspaper. Ann has walked the Freedom Trail many times.